The OFFICIAL NOTTINGHAM FOREST ANNUAL 2013

Contributors: John Lawson, Fraser Nicholson, Ben White, Cheryl McCluskey, Tom Crosse, Nick Richardson.
Designed by: Jane Greig

A Grange Publication

© 2012. Published by Grange Communications Ltd., Edinburgh, under licence from Nottingham Forest. Printed in the EU.

Photographs © Action Images

ISBN no. 978-1-908925-12-1

£7.99

anny Sonner	N. Ireland	2004
arlon King	Jamaica	2004-06
ammy Clingan	N. Ireland	2006-08
unior Agogo	Ghana	2006-08
Robert Earnshaw	Wales	2008-
Chris Gunter	Wales	2009-
Radoslaw Majewski	Poland	2009-
Lee Camp	N. Ireland	2011-

HONOURS BOARD

FOOTBALL LEAGUE
Division One
Champions 1977-78 and 1997-98
Runners-up 1966-67 and 1978-79

Division Two
Champions 1906-07 and 1921-22
Runners-up 1956-57

League One
Runners-up 2007-08

Division Three (South)
Champions 1950-51

F.A. CUP
Winners 1898 and 1959
Runners-up 1991

FOOTBALL LEAGUE CUP
Winners 1978, 1979, 1989
and 1990
Runners-up 1980 and 1982

EUROPEAN CUP
Winners 1979 and 1980

EUROPEAN SUPER CUP
Winners 1979-80
Runners-up 1980-81

SIMOD CUP
Winners 1989

ZENITH DATA SYSTEMS CUP
Winners 1992

ANGLO-SCOTTISH CUP
Winners 1977

CHARITY SHIELD
Winners 1978
Runners-up 1959

CONTENTS

NEW SIGNINGS

The City Ground faithful were granted their wish when new manager Sean O'Driscoll made the first moves to rebuild the Nottingham Forest side this season.

With several players, like skipper Luke Chambers, leaving the club, there was a need to bring in fresh faces once the takeover had taken place.

And the first signing brought crowd favourite Adlene Guedioura back to Nottingham in a permanent move from Wolves.

He had been on loan the previous season and in his 19 games had caught the eye with his commitment and creativity in the middle of the field.

And the fans' approval at the deal was echoed by the player himself. He said: "I was on holiday and looking on Twitter and saw that the fans had asked me to come back.

"The fans were really good to me when I was here on loan and I really enjoyed it. I will do my best to play like I did – but I want to do even better."

Guedioura's arrival signalled the start of a glut of signings to The City Ground in the build-up to the new campaign.

He was followed soon afterwards by Danny Collins, who arrived from Stoke with a reputation of playing a big part in helping sides win promotion from the Championship.

The experienced defender won promotion twice with Sunderland and helped West Ham win back their Premier League status while on loan last season.

Forest then ended their seemingly endless search for a permanent left back when Dan Harding, who had figured in Southampton's promotion surge last season, was signed in a permanent deal.

The former England Under 21 international said: "I'm really excited about the move. Forest are a massive club, which is

hopefully going in the right direction."

More experience and versatility was recruited when Greg Halford made the move from troubled Portsmouth and he was convinced that it was the right career move for him.

He said: "This is the right time for me to be at Forest. The facilities are great and I know the owners have big plans to develop the club."

Midfielder Simon Gillett, a player well-known to O'Driscoll from their days together at Doncaster, was next to join the Forest bandwagon after his deal with the Yorkshire club had come to an end.

And he made no secret of the fact that he was keen to join up with his former manager again. "The manager played a massively important part in me wanting to come here. I know the way he works and I feel he can get the best out of me."

Gillett was quickly followed through The City Ground door by Spanish defender Daniel Ayala, who arrived in a season-long loan from Norwich City, where he had moved from Liverpool.

He commented: "I know all about Forest and their history as twice winners of the European Cup and this is a great opportunity for me."

O'Driscoll then boosted his strike force by signing Republic of Ireland international Simon Cox from West Brom.

Cox, who made his name as a free-scoring front player with Swindon, said: "I'm really excited about the new challenge. I met the Chairman and could tell that it's a club going forward."

And the signings continued when 23 year old defender Sam Hutchinson – he can play at right back or in the middle of the back four - signed a season-long loan from Chelsea.

PLAYER FACTS

CHRIS COHEN

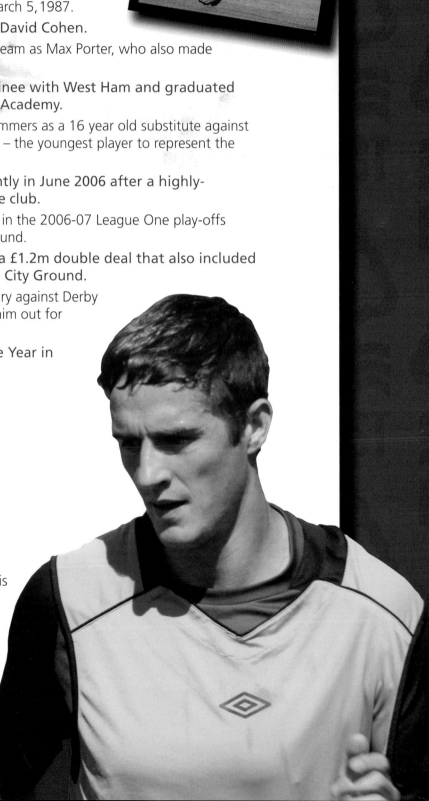

- He was born in Norwich on March 5, 1987.
- His full name is Christopher David Cohen.
- He played in the same school team as Max Porter, who also made it into the professional game.
- He began his career as a trainee with West Ham and graduated from their highly-respected Academy.
- He made his debut for The Hammers as a 16 year old substitute against Sunderland in December 2003 – the youngest player to represent the club in 80 years.
- Yeovil signed him permanently in June 2006 after a highly-successful loan spell with the club.
- He helped Yeovil defeat Forest in the 2006-07 League One play-offs before moving to The City Ground.
- He linked up with Forest in a £1.2m double deal that also included Arron Davies moving to The City Ground.
- He suffered a serious knee injury against Derby in September 2011 that kept him out for the remainder of last season.
- He was Forest's Player of the Year in the 2008-09 season.

FAVOURITES:

Ground: Wembley
Player: Steven Gerrard
Sportsman: Tiger Woods
Food: Sausage and mash
Car: Range Rover
TV Programme: The Sopranos
Film: The Godfather
Album: Definitely Maybe by Oasis
Place to visit: Dubai
Game played in: West Brom, January 2009

MANAGER – SEAN O'DRISCOLL

Sean O'Driscoll became Nottingham Forest's fourth manager in little over a year with the promise to uphold the club's proud tradition of playing the game in an attractive manner.

In his managerial career with Bournemouth and Doncaster, O'Driscoll had earned a reputation for encouraging his teams to play a passing game that was easy on the eye.

And those principles fit in neatly at Forest, where successive teams played an open and attractive style of play long before the heady days of Brian Clough's 18-year reign by the Trent.

And within hours of his appointment at The City Ground, he revealed: "I fully understand and appreciate the tradition of the club and let's say straight away that this is a great place to play football.

"I know there is a Forest way of playing and we need to keep that in mind but there is not just one way of playing. The best way is the right way.

"I know from my days coming here with Bournemouth and Doncaster that Forest supporters appreciate good football and opposing teams enjoy playing at The City Ground because they know it is a sheer pleasure.

"I also know that Forest playing at home can be a formidable force and I would like us to be in a position where we are recreating the full houses of 30,000 with supporters appreciating winning football."

O'Driscoll's former role at the club was more about safeguarding their Championship status than producing the flowing football for which he was renowned.

He arrived last January as assistant manager to Steve Cotterill as Forest attempted to move away from the dreaded relegation zone.

They achieved that and when the club's new owners went looking for a new manager following Cotterill's departure, the impact O'Driscoll had made during the second half of the 2011-12 season was clearly noted.

But when he was unveiled as the new manager he made no lavish promises to turn Forest from relegation candidates to promotion possibles in quick-fire time.

He added: "I am a process manager not an outcome manager. I am a firm believer that it is all about trying to do the right things bit by bit. There are times when they might not work but if we can get supporters believing in what we are trying to achieve then it will hopefully lead to the results that we all want to see."

WHO AM I?

Here are photos of some of the players, but they've gone fuzzy! Can you figure out who they are from the information from their profiles on the website?

< My Forest debut was against Barnsley in 2009
< I was born in 1986
< My position is centre forward
< I scored 8 goals for The Reds last season
< I am 185cm tall
< I had a serious knee injury which kept me out of the game for over a year

My Forest debut was against Port Vale >
I was born in 1987 >
I play in the centre of midfield >
I joined Forest from Yeovil Town in 2007 >
I am 178cm tall >
I was forced to miss the majority of last season > through a serious knee injury

< My Forest debut was against Reading
< I was born in 1985
< I play in the centre of midfield
< I made 33 league appearances for The Reds last season
< I am 187cm tall
< My early career was spent with French side Angers

My Forest debut was against Sheffield United > in 2000
I was born in 1982 >
I play on the left side of midfield >
I have been capped by my country Republic > of Ireland 27 times
I am 170cm tall >
This is my second spell with Forest >

For the best part of 40 years everywhere you have seen the name of Nottingham Forest, a now-famous symbol has stood by its side.

The easily recognised Forest tree is now known the world over as the emblem for the famous club.

It was adopted in 1973 when the search began for a new Forest badge to take over from Nottingham's Coat of Arms that was previously used by the club.

The Coat of Arms had been used since 1957 and two years later was prominently featured on the players' shirts when they won the FA Cup by defeating Luton Town 2-1 at Wembley.

But there was always a desire by the club to have their very own identity and in 1973 a competition was organised in the Nottingham Evening Post to find a new club crest.

More than 800 people entered the competition and the judges decided on the design put forward by David Lewis, who was a designer/ lecturer at Nottingham's Trent Polytechnic.

He explained at the time: "The tree was taken as the most appropriate subject to symbolise Forest.

"It was found to be too complicated if more than one tree was used but too weak and vague with a tree on its own.

"The heraldic treatment of water provided a more unique quality as well as giving a strong base to the design – water being appropriate because of The City Ground's proximity to the River Trent.

"These points were important if supporters were to build strong emotional ties with the badge.

"The overall proportion was arrived at after a great deal of experimentation. It was decided that a stylised tree shape was more appropriate than any particular species of tree. Shape, however, had to be strong and individual."

So there you have it.

In 1973 the new badge was adopted and since then has appeared thousands – if not millions – of times in print, on buildings, shirts and leisurewear to give the name of Nottingham Forest an everlasting identity.

Garath McCleary moved on to start a new Premier League career with Reading last summer – but not before he had made his mark on our history.

He was named as Player of the Year for 2011-12 and in doing so joined a long list of illustrious names from our past.

Players like Kenny Burns, Peter Shilton, Nigel Clough, Des Walker and, of course, Stuart Pearce have claimed the title in years past and McCleary was understandably delighted to put his name alongside those greats.

He said: "To be perfectly honest it is something that I never expected, particularly when the season got underway.

"Back then I was not even fit after recovering from a knee operation and I had a job to force myself into the side.

"I didn't get a chance to show Steve McClaren what I could do but it all changed for me when Steve Cotterill became manager.

"I needed a manager to back me and give me an opportunity and that's what Steve Cotterill did. I always knew I could make an impact but if I am honest I didn't think it would go as well for me as it did.

"But considering that I didn't start playing until last December, it was superb. Obviously it was great for me but the important thing was that I played a part in helping Forest stay up because that was the important challenge.

It was a far cry from the times when the young winger, who joined us from Bromley in 2008, struggled to get a look in during Billy Davies' time as manager.

But he took on the challenge

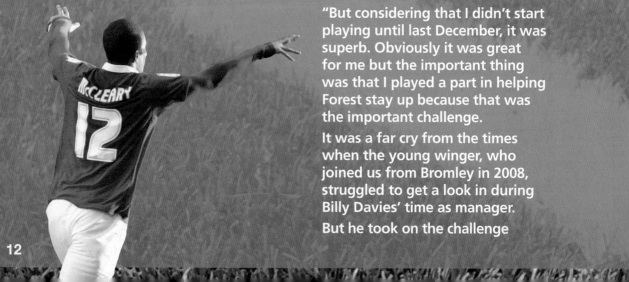

OF THE YEAR

and ended up by pipping Dexter Blackstock and Radi Majewski as our top scorer for the season.

Four of those goals came in an unforgettable night against Leeds United at Elland Road when we enjoyed a spectacular 7-3 win.

He added: "It was just incredible. Everything I seemed to hit went in the back of the net and I don't think I'll have another game like that.

"I got the match ball from the game and together with the Player of the Year award, they will be reminders of a fabulous period in my career."

The last ten winners of the Forest Player of the Year award are:

2011-12	Garath McCleary
2010-11	Luke Chambers
2009-10	Lee Camp
2008-09	Chris Cohen
2007-08	Julian Bennett
2006-07	Grant Holt
2005-06	Ian Breckin
2004-05	Paul Gerrard
2003-04	Andy Reid
2002-03	David Johnson

CLUB

★★★★★★★★★

CUP VICTORY:
14-0 v Clapton (away), FA Cup first round, January 17 1891

POINTS (TWO FOR A WIN):
70 in Division Three (South), 1950-51

ATTENDANCE:
49,946 v Manchester United in Division One, October 28 1967

POINTS (THREE FOR A WIN):
94 in Division One, 1997-98

RECEIPTS:
£499,099 v Bayern Munich in UEFA Cup quarter final, second leg, March 19 1996

LEAGUE GOALS:
110 in Division Three (South), 1950-51

MOST CAPPED PLAYER:
76 by Stuart Pearce for England

LEAGUE VICTORY:
12-0 v Leicester Fosse, Division One, April 12 1909

MOST LEAGUE APPEARANCES:
614 by Bob McKinlay between 1951-70

YOUNGEST LEAGUE PLAYER:
Craig Westcarr, 16 years 257 days v Burnley on October 13 2001

TRANSFER FEE RECEIVED:
£8.5m from Liverpool for Stan Collymore, June 1995

TRANSFER FEE PAID:
£3.5m to Glasgow Celtic for Pierre van Hooijdonk, March 1997

LEAGUE SCORER IN A SEASON:
36 by Wally Ardron in Division Three (South) 1950-51

LEAGUE GOALS IN AGGREGATE:
199 by Grenville Morris from 1898-1913

RECORDS

GOALS IN ONE MATCH:
4 by 12 players

Enoch West v Sunderland (h), November 9 1907

Tommy Gibson v Burnley (a), January 12 1913

Tom Peacock v Port Vale (h), December 23 1933

Tom Peacock v Barnsley (h), November 9 1935

Tom Peacock v Port Vale (h), November 23 1935

Tom Peacock v Doncaster Rovers (h), December 16 1952

Tommy Capel v Gillingham (h), November 18 1950

Wally Ardron v Hull City (h), December 26 1952

Tommy Wilson v Barnsley (h), February 9 1957

Peter Withe v Ipswich Town (h),

October 4 1977

Marlon Harewood v Stoke City (h), February 22 2003

Garath McCleary v Leeds United (a), March 20 2012

CONSECUTIVE LEAGUE WINS:
7 from May 9 1979 to September 1 1979

CONSECUTIVE LEAGUE DEFEATS:
14 from March 21 1913 to September 27 1913

CONSECUTIVE LEAGUE DRAWS:
7 from April 29 1978 to September 1 1978

CONSECUTIVE UNBEATEN LEAGUE MATCHES:
42 from November 26 1977 to November 25 1978

CONSECUTIVE GAMES WITHOUT A LEAGUE WIN:
19 from September 8 1998 to January 16 1999

15

FOREST QUIZ

1 Who was Forest's top scorer in the 2011-12 season?

2 Which Forest player joined Leicester City midway through last season?

3 Which Forest player signed for Forest from Fulham in the summer of 2011?

4 Which European Cup winner became chairman of Nottingham Forest during the course of last season?

5 What was the name of the former England manager who was in charge of Forest for a spell last season?

6 Which Forest player was injured against Derby County in September 2011 and missed the rest of the season?

7 Who was Lee Camp's No. 2 for most of last season?

8 Which international team does our former full back Chris Gunter play for?

9 Which Dutch club did Steve McClaren rejoin after leaving Forest as manager last season?

10 Can you name the five players Forest had on loan last season?

11 Which club did Steve Cotterill manage before moving to The City Ground?

12 What nationality is Radi Majewski?

13 Who scored Forest's first league goal last season?

14 Garath McCleary scored four goals in Forest's 7-3 win over Leeds in March. Who scored the other goals?

15 Who was Forest's only ever present player in league games last season?

16 Who was Forest's Player of the Year in the 2011-12 season?

17 Who scored Forest's goals in the 1979 and 1980 European Cup finals?

18 Who beat Forest in the semi final of the 2010-11 Championship play-offs?

19 From which club did Forest sign Ishmael Miller in August 2011?

20 What is the name of the stand opposite the Main Stand at The City Ground?

Answers on P61.

PLAYER FACTS

GUY MOUSSI

- He was born in Bondy, Seine-Saint-Denis January 23, 1985.
- He began his career with Angers SCO in his native France.
- He spent six seasons with Angers and played in 120 games.
- He signed for Forest in June 2008.
- His first game was against Reading on August 10.
- He received his second booking for over-enthusiastically celebrating his first goal in England against Barnsley and was subsequently sent off.
- He had five months out of action in his first full season following a serious knee ligament injury.
- In the summer of 2011 he signed a new three year contract at The City Ground.
- He's always been a midfielder but injuries led to him playing in defence for Forest last season.
- He has a sister who has also come over from France and lives in Dunstable.

FAVOURITES:

Ground: St. James' Park Newcastle

Player: Zinedine Zidane

Sportsman: Muhammad Ali

Food: Thieboudienne

Car: Bentley Continental

TV Programme: Fresh Prince of Bel Air

Film: Man on Fire

Album: Mauvais Oeil by Lunatic

Place to visit: Copacabana, Rio de Janeiro

Game played in: Derby, January 2011

SEASON REVIEW 2011-12

Sat 17th Sept 2011 vs Derby County

AUGUST

There were many new faces on the Forest scene when the season began in early August.

Manager Billy Davies had departed and as well as having former England manager Steve McClaren and a new backroom team, we also paraded new signings in the shape of Jonathan Greening, George Boateng, Matt Derbyshire and Ishmael Miller as well as old favourite Andy Reid.

Three of the new faces were in the side that kicked off the season with a disappointing goalless draw against Barnsley in front of an expectant City Ground crowd.

And the lack of goals was a common theme as the first month of the season progressed in stuttering style.

We lost 2-0 at Millwall in our opening away game of the Championship programme with Darius Henderson opening the scoring and Liam Trotter adding a second in the second half.

But we responded to that setback with our first goal – from Chris Gunter – and first win in a 1-0 victory over Doncaster Rovers at The Keepmoat Stadium.

Said Gunter:"People can stop talking about us not having got that first win now. We have had a few new boys come into the side and it will take time for things to happen."

We fell 2-0 behind at home to Leicester in the next game following goals by David Nugent and Gelson Fernandes. But there was a cause for optimism in the way we fought back with a penalty from Lewis McGugan and Boateng's first goal for the club that clinched a 2-2 draw against our big spending East Midlands neighbours.

But the month ended in a demoralising home defeat by relegated West Ham on a day when McClaren's men were largely outplayed in a 4-1 defeat in front of the SKY cameras.

There was an element of good fortune about The Hammers' first goal when Matt Taylor's shot struck Luke Chambers and left Lee Camp stranded but after that West Ham underlined their billing as promotion favourites with further goals from Kevin Nolan, Carlton Cole and Winston Reid. Robbie Findley scored our consolation goal.

SEPTEMBER

We badly needed to bring some stability to performances and results but with games against high-flying Southampton and arch rivals Derby County to start the month, it wasn't going to be easy. And so it proved.

We were right out of luck at St. Mary's Stadium as The Saints survived a series of penalty appeals that left Steve McClaren bewildered and frustrated.

Matt Derbyshire's first goal for the club gave us the lead but two goals by freescoring Ricky Lambert put Southampton ahead before Radi Majewski produced an equaliser.

We continued to have a big say in the game but it was Southampton who clinched victory when Lambert completed his hat-trick with a header seven minutes from time.

Said Derbyshire: "We could easily have had three penalties. Ishmael Miller had one claim in the first half and I had two in the second.

"I am lost for words but it is very disappointing – not just for me but the whole team."

There was more drama in our first East Midlands derby of the season against Derby – starting in the first minute when their goalkeeper Frank Fielding was sent off for flattening Miller in the box and leaving Reid to give us the lead from the penalty spot.

Jamie Ward equalised for Derby just before the half hour at a time when our midfielder Chris Cohen was lying injured in the Rams' half with a knee ligament injury that was to bring an end to his campaign with the season only weeks old.

Derby's ten men went on to grab a 73rd minute winner through Jeff Hendrick and we knew it wasn't going to be our day when skipper Luke Chambers headed over the bar in injury time.

And Chambers admitted: "We know we let our fans down very badly. It's going to be some time before I can wipe out the memory of a defeat like that."

By the time we played our next league game against Watford we had recruited the services of Queens Park Rangers' defender Clint Hill on loan and he played a crucial part in getting us back to winning ways when Miller scored the only goal of the game at Watford.

But the month ended in disastrous fashion as we crashed 5-1 to Burnley at Turf Moor. We were 4-0 down at half-time and although Miller scored for the second successive game, it was Burnley's night as they romped to a comfortable win.

OCTOBER

Ishmael Miller also scored in the next game against Birmingham City at The City Ground on what turned out to be a day of reckoning.

After the 3-1 defeat manager Steve McClaren announced he was resigning as manager after only 13 competitive games in charge.

But as the fallout continued our owner Nigel Doughty announced that he was standing down as Chairman, leaving the club to secure the appointments of two key figures at a time when we were struggling so badly on the field.

15th Oct 2011 Steve Cotterill becomes manager

Former player Frank Clark accepted the offer to become the new Chairman and one of his first acts was to oversee the appointment of Portsmouth boss Steve Cotterill as the new manager at The City Ground.

He watched the next game, which saw us lose 1-0 at Coventry, but took charge for the first time when we entertained Middlesbrough the following Tuesday.

Goals by Marcus Tudgay and Lewis McGugan saw his reign get off to the perfect start with a 2-0 win that also brought an end to the Championship's only unbeaten record of the season.

The new manager had provided a spark and McGugan reflected: "Everyone could see the confidence running through the side.

"We all put in maximum effort and it showed. It was a really good team performance."

It got better in the next game when we became only the second team of the season to beat Blackpool on their own ground.

Wes Morgan gave us the lead and although evergreen striker Kevin Phillips equalised just before half-time, Majewski pounced for the winner.

Guy Moussi became our first player to be sent off in the season after being shown a second yellow card nine minutes from time but we held out to register an important win.

Unfortunately we couldn't make it three wins out of three against Hull City on a day when Greg Cunningham made his debut on loan from Manchester City.

The winner came from former Peterborough striker Aaron McLean 15 minutes from time.

NOVEMBER

It was important for us to bounce back from the Hull setback and three days later we did just that when Marcus Tudgay got the winner against Reading at The City Ground.

For long periods there was nothing in the game and in the first half in particular we failed to get into any kind of rhythm.

But there was a distinct improvement in the second half and in the 75th minute Chambers ventured forward to supply the cross from which Tudgay fired past Reading keeper Adam Federici.

Our inconsistency reared its head in the next game when we lost 3-0 to

Steve Cotterill's former club at Fratton Park.

Although we had chances throughout the game we failed to profit from any of them while Norwegian Erik Huseklepp scored twice for Portsmouth either side of a header from Dave Kitson.

Back at The City Ground we showed fighting qualities to come back from twice being behind to Ipswich to score twice in the last six minutes and register a dramatic 3-2 win over The Tractor Boys.

Ipswich defender Danny Collins headed Ipswich in front and although Robbie Findley equalised from close range, Collins put the visitors ahead again just after the hour mark.

But we were back in business when Joel Lynch headed his first goal for us from Andy Reid's cross and in an eventful finale, Tudgay headed past David Stockdale in the last minute to give us our fourth victory in six games following Cotterill's arrival.

We did enough to earn something from the next game at promotion-chasing Cardiff but a 70th minute goal by substitute Joe Mason proved crucial as we went down 1-0 in South Wales.

Worse followed three days later at The City Ground as Leeds swept to a 4-0 win when nothing went right for us.

Goals by Robert Snodgrass and Jonny Howson gave Leeds a first half grip and although Cotterill made half-time changes in a bid to change the course of the game, Luciano Becchio headed a third four minutes after the break and Adam Clayton rounded off the perfect night for the Elland Road side.

DECEMBER

We had not scored for three hours as we entered December but that spell without a goal was to stretch to incredible lengths as we struggled to make any impact in the last month of the year.

We didn't score a single goal throughout five games that month and our only point came from a goalless draw against Bristol City at Ashton Gate.

But before that we went down to successive 1-0 defeats at Brighton and at home to Dougie Freedman's Crystal Palace.

We were right out of luck against Brighton, where we produced some of our best football of the season to date, but were dealt a cruel late blow.

Brighton had not threatened our goal until the 90th minute when Will Buckley had made the most of the one shooting chance to come their way.

Said Jonathan Greening: "We put in a really good shift against a strong Brighton side who had been doing really well.

"I can't believe we have lost – we had so many chances to win the game but just couldn't put them away and then get punished very late in the game."

We slipped to our fourth successive defeat at The City Ground a week later when Glenn Murray's 57th minute strike earned Palace victory.

There was some consolation for us in that the game marked the eagerly-awaited return of Dexter Blackstock after 12 months out recovering from a serious knee injury.

He said: "I was very happy to be back out there even though it would have been nice to have seen us get a better result.

"It was a great feeling and I am ready to play my part. I am waiting for my chance."

He started the following

23

game against Bristol City but it was Marcus Tudgay who promised to provide us with a goal and much-needed points.

But time after time he was denied by former England keeper David James but at least the performance was a good one and represented the first clean sheet since Steve Cotterill took over.

Our goal drought continued and on Boxing Day we were punished by our former loan striker George Boyd as Peterborough pulled off a 1-0 win at The City Ground.

He struck with a superb lob in the 28th minute and when we failed to find a way past goalkeeper Joe Lewis, it turned out to be another highly frustrating afternoon.

Our tale of woe went on, however, when a 58th minute goal by Scotland striker Kenny Miller earned Cardiff City a 1-0 City Ground win in the final match of 2011.

Our cause was not helped when we lost Robbie Findley with a shoulder injury in the early minutes of the game but we had to find an answer to a goalscoring problem that stretched back to seven games.

JANUARY

We started 2012 desperately in need of a boost after seven games without a goal – never mind a win.

But it all came to an end against the side who had provided our last goals and victory – Ipswich.

We went to Portman Road and eased to a 3-1 win that ended our ten and a half hour search for a goal.

Marcus Tudgay opened the scoring in the fifth minute and Garath McCleary made it 2-0 midway through the first half. Ipswich pulled a goal back through a Grant Leadbitter penalty 15 minutes from time but any late nerves we might have had were swept away when Tudgay headed his second goal

Tues 31st Jan 2012 vs Burnley

and our third three minutes later.

Skipper Luke Chambers said: "It's easy to say that result was coming but we genuinely felt it to be the case.

"We didn't look like a side short on confidence and the quality of the goals we scored was outstanding."

It went wrong for Chambers – and us – in the following game when our skipper was sent off just four minutes into the second half with Southampton already leading by a 26th minute goal from Guy Do Prado.

On a day when Marlon Harewood made his reappearance for us on a short-term contract, we had created plenty of openings early in the game but David Connolly and Morgan Schneiderlin went on to add more goals against our ten men and make sure The Saints completed the double over us.

Southampton's title rivals at the time West Ham were next up in what turned out to be Wes Morgan's last game for the club before leaving for Leicester.

Once more we produced a battling performance with no lack of flair but were right out of luck as West Ham benefitted from two penalty decisions to take a 2-0 lead before Lewis McGugan pulled a goal back in the last minute.

By the time we played our next league game against Burnley at home, we had signed midfielder Adlene Guedioura on loan from Wolves and he made his debut alongside teenager Jamaal Lascelles.

But we were on the receiving end once again as Jay Rodriguez scored twice and could easily have had a hat-trick.

FEBRUARY

Before we played our first game in February the club was in shock at the sudden death of owner Nigel Doughty on the day we were scheduled to play Derby at Pride Park.

The game had been postponed because of the wintry conditions outside the ground but even a week later when we entertained Watford, there was an air of disbelief at the terribly sad events of a week earlier.

We took the lead in the game with a superb goal from McCleary on a day when we had three more debutants in loan signings Danny Higginbotham, George Elokobi and Scott Wootton.

But Watford equalised through Troy Deeney just before half-time and although we created a host of chances we failed to get the winner that we deserved.

Said Guedioura: "We were close to winning the game and showed the fans that we have a good team.

"It was good to create so many chances and we should have scored more goals but step by step I think we will show a good face of Nottingham Forest."

Goals immediately before and after half-time by Marvin Emnes and Lukas Jutkiewicz put Middlesbrough in control of our next game at The Riverside Stadium but the introduction of substitute Andy Reid transformed us and Joel Lynch headed us back into the game in the 66th minute.

But despite increasing pressure on the Boro goal we failed to get the equaliser and the need for survival points was getting more acute by the week.

Before the month was out, however, we produced vital wins over Coventry and Birmingham that were to give us the belief that we would move towards safety.

With Coventry also in the thick of the relegation battle it was crucial that we defeated the Sky Blues at The City Ground but we left it late with goals by Garath McCleary and Robbie Findley coming in the last 16 minutes of a tension-filled game.

We became the first team to win at Birmingham in the league all season and our 2-1 success owed much to two goals from Dexter Blackstock as he continued his comeback in stunning style. He put us ahead and although Chris Burke equalised, Blackstock fired a second following a fine piece of control.

Sat 18th Feb 2012 vs Coventry

25

MARCH

Garath McCleary continued his excellent run of form by scoring in our next game at Barnsley but we had to settle for a point in a 1-1 draw after Craig Davies had fired home a spectacular equaliser.

Unfortunately, our mini revival that had seen us take seven points from three games came to a halt when we lost 2-1 at home to Doncaster, who themselves were fighting for every point.

A superb strike by Frederic Piquionne gave the visitors the lead, which Kyle Bennett increased just after the break and although Dexter Blackstock gave us a lifeline, there was no way back for us on the night.

Our rollercoaster ride continued as we defeated Millwall at The City Ground on an afternoon when Andy Reid turned in a match-winning display.

He created the opening two goals for McCleary and Danny Higginbotham and after Darius Henderson had put Millwall back in the game, Reid settled it with a dipping 25 yard shot past goalkeeper David Forde.

Said Reid: "The most important thing is that we have taken the three points and held firm under pressure to prevent Millwall getting back into the game."

We were in touching distance of taking a point from our return meeting with Derby but were left empty-handed when Jake Buxton struck in the fourth minute of injury time.

It was the first time in 40 years that Derby had done the double over us in the league but we swept aside the disappointment to produce one of the most spectacular results achieved by the club for many a season.

We produced a magical performance to beat Leeds 7-3 at Elland Road and in the process McCleary wrote himself into our record books.

Sat 10th March 2012 vs Millwall

He was believed to be the first player to score four goals in an away game to take his tally to eight in nine games as we played our most irrepressible football of the season against Neil Warnock's side.

Adlene Guedioura had opened the scoring with what turned out to be our Goal of the Season and Blackstock also scored twice as we ran riot.

Said Blackstock: "Garath has been our main man in recent weeks to help us climb out of trouble. His performance was incredible and he richly deserved all the praise that came his way."

We left it very late to earn our next point in a 1-1 home draw with Brighton after Sam Vokes had given the visitors the lead just after the hour mark.

But Brighton old boy Lynch turned in his third goal of the season after Marcus Tudgay had headed a Reid free-kick into the danger area.

We moved five points clear of the relegation places with a hard-earned point in a goalless draw at Leicester.

And we strengthened our position still further against Crystal Palace when Radi Majewski scored a brilliant hat-trick in a 3-0 win.

It was the first three-goal blitz of his career and all of his goals came in the second half. Afterwards he said: "I did not expect to get the three goals, particularly at half-time when the gaffer asked me when I was going to join the party!"

APRIL

Our revival, which had seen us claim eight points from a possible 12, came to an end when we were beaten 1-0 at home by Bristol City.

Chris Wood scored the only goal from the penalty spot but just as important for the visitors were the string of saves made by goalkeeper Dean Gerken to keep us at bay.

We overcame that disappointment to bounce back with a 1-0 win at Peterborough thanks to a first half goal by Dexter Blackstock.

We could have had more to show for our dominance but even when Garath McCleary was controversially red carded in the 65th minute we had little cause for concern as we picked up three precious points.

Another superb goalkeeping display against us – this time by Blackpool's Matt Gilks – left us having to settle for a point in a goalless home draw against Ian Holloway's men.

But our survival was assured after the next game at Reading – even though we lost 1-0 to a side clinching their place in the Premier League.

Results elsewhere dictated that we could not finish in the bottom three but despite the relief, we were disappointed not to take anything from a game that was won by Mikele Leigertwood's 81st minute goal.

Our final away game of the season epitomised much of our season as good fortune eluded us in a 2-1 defeat by Hull at The KC Stadium.

An own goal by Chris Gunter and a debatable penalty – awarded against Chambers - by Matty Fryatt gave Hull a fortunate 2-0 lead before Radi Majewski scored a consolation goal in the last minute.

But we finished a topsy-turvy season on a high note with a welcome home win over Cotterill's old club Portsmouth.

Blackstock scored both goals in the second half to take his tally to eight in 16 starts and reaffirm his status as one of the best strikers outside of the Premiership.

Summing up the season manager Steve Cotterill said: "One of our biggest problems was that we didn't have a defence for half the season, certainly while I have been here.

"But we also had to deal with the fact that we didn't have a striker who was capable of making a difference by scoring goals in tight games.

"When you put the two together it is a recipe for disaster but we brought defenders in on loan and Dexter has come back and done exceptionally well."

Sat 14th April 2012 vs Blackpool

CUP GAMES REVIEW

Carling Cup

We began our Carling Cup campaign against city neighbours Notts County in a tie that turned out to be one of the most memorable of Nottingham derbies.

It needed a penalty shoot-out to determine the winners but the 120 minutes that went before that were full of dramatic twists and turns.

County were in charge for most of the night with Mike Edwards giving them a 16th minute lead before the game swung our way with goals by Lewis McGugan and Robbie Findley.

Our former striker Craig Westcarr equalised in the 76th minute and extra-time brought what seemed to be the winner from veteran striker Lee Hughes.

But cometh the hour, cometh Wes Morgan with a bullet shot in the last minute of extra-time to send the tie into penalties.

The tension continued but the shoot-out swung our way when Luke Chambers' penalty gave us the edge and Notts skipper Neal Bishop fired over as we won 4-3 on penalties.

The second round was much more clear-cut as we eased to a 4-1 victory over League One Wycombe Wanderers.

We scored twice in the opening seven minutes through Ishmael Miller and a McGugan penalty and added to the lead in the 62nd minute through Findley. Elliot Benyon reduced the deficit soon

afterwards but Radi Majewski put the seal on an excellent night.

The game also marked the first team debut of Kieron Freeman, who came on as a substitute and was denied a goal by Wycombe keeper Nikki Bull.

That earned us a third round tie against Newcastle United at The City Ground on what turned out to be another memorable cup game.

Newcastle twice took the lead in normal time through Peter Lovenkrands but on both occasions Findley and Matt Derbyshire forced an equaliser.

The Geordies once again took the lead in extra-time through full back Danny Simpson but back we came for Marcus Tudgay to set up a thrilling finale.

But it was Newcastle who edged it when skipper Fabricio Coloccini headed the winner from a cross by former Manchester United winger Gabriel Obertan.

Our players had given an excellent account of themselves and Findley reflected the mood in The Reds' camp when he said: "The result was disappointing but all the players did really well and gave everything they had.

"It was just a pity the game didn't finish the way we wanted."

FA Cup

We were matched with East Midlands rivals Leicester City in the third round of the FA Cup and it was honours even after the first game at The City Ground.

It was very much a game of two halves with us having the best of the opening half and then Leicester shading it after half-time.

Kieron Freeman made his full debut as we started brightly but as the game wore on City came more into it and deserved to take the tie to a second game at The King Power Stadium.

The replay turned out to be one of the worst nights of the season as Leicester seized the initiative from an early stage and never let go.

An Own goal by George Boateng set them on their way after just six minutes before Jermaine Beckford added a second on the half hour.

The former Leeds and Everton striker prospered further in the second half, scoring two more in the space of seven minutes to complete his hat-trick.

As full back Chris Gunter admitted: "It was a horrible night. We can't forget what happened against Leicester but we've got to move on because something has to change."

WORDSEARCH

Find the words in the grid. Words can go horizontally, vertically and diagonally in all eight directions. Answers on P61.

BLACKSTOCK
CLOUGH
MAJEWSKI
COHEN
MOUSSI
CITY GROUND
TRENT END
REID
ROBIN
MARIAN
CAMP
DUGOUT
TUDGAY
FINDLEY
FOREST

A	B	C	C	I	T	Y	G	R	O	U	N	D	C	N	E
K	L	I	B	D	R	E	A	D	A	A	O	I	I	A	S
I	A	T	D	I	E	R	R	U	E	K	D	W	T	I	H
I	C	G	S	R	N	D	T	G	D	R	G	I	Y	R	A
S	K	D	A	T	T	M	O	R	U	I	E	P	M	A	C
B	S	A	L	Y	E	N	S	P	G	N	R	L	G	M	R
L	T	O	K	B	N	O	I	M	O	B	I	L	E	R	D
A	O	N	M	A	D	I	D	N	U	L	S	F	E	O	H
C	C	L	O	U	G	H	E	L	T	U	D	G	A	Y	A
K	K	Z	U	W	G	V	Y	H	I	F	A	I	Z	B	C
F	P	M	S	E	H	T	M	G	O	B	L	N	E	I	D
G	I	N	S	F	E	R	D	R	U	C	R	D	R	N	C
T	I	F	I	N	D	L	E	Y	R	K	A	O	L	T	O
R	A	O	T	N	R	S	W	D	O	Y	D	Y	B	A	H
A	M	E	C	U	T	A	Q	E	B	E	K	O	D	I	E
E	L	E	B	W	N	M	A	J	E	W	S	K	I	K	N

SPOT THE DIFFERENCE

Can you spot 5 differences between these two pictures? Answers on P61.

Date	Opponent	Score	Scorers
Sat Aug 6	BARNSLEY	0-0	
Tue Aug 9	NOTTS COUNTY (CC1)	3-3*	McGugan, Findley, Morgan
Sat Aug 13	Millwall	0-2	
Tue Aug 16	Doncaster Rovers	1-0	Gunter
Sat Aug 20	LEICESTER CITY	2-2	McGugan (pen) Boateng
Tue Aug 23	Wycombe Wanderers (CC2)	4-1	Miller, McGugan (pen), Findley, Majewski
Sun Aug 28	WEST HAM UNITED	1-4	Findley
Sat Sep 10	Southampton	2-3	Derbyshire, Majewski
Sat Sep 17	DERBY COUNTY	1-2	Reid (pen)
Tue Sep 20	NEWCASTLE UNITED (CC3)	3-4**	Findley, Derbyshire, Tudgay
Sat Sep 24	Watford	1-0	Miller
Tue Sep 27	Burnley	1-5	Miller
Sun Oct 2	BIRMINGHAM CITY	1-3	Miller
Sat Oct 15	Coventry City	0-1	
Tue Oct 18	MIDDLESBROUGH	2-0	Tudgay, McGugan
Sat Oct 22	Blackpool	2-1	Morgan, Majewski
Sat Oct 29	HULL CITY	0-1	
Tue Nov 1	READING	1-0	Tudgay
Sat Nov 5	Portsmouth	0-3	
Sat Nov 19	IPSWICH TOWN	3-2	Findley, Lynch, Tudgay
Sat Nov 26	Cardiff City	0-1	
Tue Nov 29	LEEDS UNITED	0-4	
Sat Dec 3	Brighton	0-1	
Sat Dec 10	CRYSTAL PALACE	0-1	
Sat Dec 17	Bristol City	0-0	
Mon Dec 26	PETERBOROUGH UNITED	0-1	
Sat Dec 31	CARDIFF CITY	0-1	
Mon Jan 2	Ipswich Town	3-1	Tudgay 2, McCleary
Sat Jan 7	LEICESTER CITY (FA3)	0-0	
Sat Jan 14	SOUTHAMPTON	0-3	
Tue Jan 17	Leicester City (FA3R)	0-4	
Sat Jan 21	West Ham United	1-2	McGugan
Tue Jan 31	BURNLEY	0-2	
Sat Feb 11	WATFORD	1-1	McCleary
Tue Feb 14	Middlesbrough	1-2	Lynch
Sat Feb 18	COVENTRY CITY	2-0	McCleary, Findley
Sat Feb 25	Birmingham City	2-1	Blackstock 2
Sat Mar 3	Barnsley	1-1	McCleary
Tue Mar 6	DONCASTER ROVERS	1-2	Blackstock
Sat Mar 10	MILLWALL	3-1	McCleary, Higginbotham, Reid
Tue Mar 13	Derby County	0-1	
Tue Mar 20	Leeds United	7-3	McCleary 4, Blackstock 2 Guedioura
Sat Mar 24	BRIGHTON	1-1	Lynch
Tue Mar 27	Leicester City	0-0	
Sat Mar 31	Crystal Palace	3-0	Majewski 3
Sat Apr 7	BRISTOL CITY	0-1	
Mon Apr 9	Peterborough United	1-0	Blackstock
Sat Apr 14	BLACKPOOL	0-0	
Tue Apr 17	Reading	0-1	
Sat Apr 21	Hull City	1-2	Majewski
Sat Apr 28	Portsmouth	2-0	Blackstock 2

NEW ERA

New Forest owners The Al Hasawi family get used to their new surroundings at The City Ground on a day when Chris Cohen, Andy Reid and Guy Moussi helped launch the new first team kit for the 2012-13 season.

New signings on parade .... Six of our summer signings Greg Halford, Daniel Ayala, Danny Collins, Dan Harding, Adlene Guedioura and Simon Gillett line-up for the cameras with two more newcomers Sam Hutchinson and Simon Cox pictured below.

ROBIN'S REDS

ROBIN'S REDS

Robin's Reds membership is changing for the 2012-13 season and it has never been better!

Depending on your age you could now join Little John's Juniors, Robin's Reds or Robin's Outlaws. Each membership has a whole range of goodies and opportunities and best of all you will be in pole position to support your favourite football club. Take a look at the full range of benefits for each membership below.

"Little John's Juniors"

For Junior Supporters aged 0-3 years and is especially for supporters who are too young to start attending games at The City Ground.

- Baby/toddler Nottingham Forest gift pack
- Personalised membership card
- Christmas card from the players
- Newsletters

"Robin's Reds"

For supporters aged 4-11 and will include all existing benefits, as well as a free under 12 Season Ticket. *

- Chance to be a match day mascot
- A joining goody bag including exclusive Robin's Reds gifts
- Christmas card from the players
- Newsletter
- Free skate hire at the National Ice Centre
- Discounts on Forest in the Community Schemes - Please call 0115 9824360 for further details
- free under 12 season ticket **
- Competitions

* purchased in conjunction with an adult Season Ticket.

**subject to age restrictions set by hosting Club.

"Robin's Outlaws"

For supporters aged 12-17. Members will receive an exclusive joining pack, including exclusive Forest headphones and a Forest sports watch.

- Match ticket priorities
- Joining goody bag
- Christmas card from the players
- Newsletter
- Discounts on Forest in the Community Schemes - Please call 0115 9824360 for further details
- Free skate hire at the National Ice Centre
- Competitions

How do you join? You can join via the Ticket Office, either in person or by calling 0871 226 1980. Calls cost 10p per minute, mobile rates may vary. You can also join by visiting www.nffcretail.com. If you have a client reference number, use this along with your surname and postcode to log in. If not, ask your mum, dad or guardian to register your details.

Once you have joined we will send your exclusive membership pack out to you in the post along with your personalised membership card. Delivery may take up to 28 days.

Please note, if you are purchasing Robin's Reds membership in order to claim the free Under 12 season ticket, you will need to provide the Ticket Office with proof of your age.

PLAYER PROFILES

Daniel Ayala

Position: Defender
Birthdate: 7/11/90
Nationality: Spanish
Forest Appearances: 0
Forest Goals: 0

The cultured Spanish defender is on a season-long loan at The City Ground from Norwich City and looking to re-establish himself in the English game after injury problems.

He joined Liverpool in September 2007 from Seville, where he had made his way through the youth team, but struggled for games in his time at Anfield. The Spanish Under 21 international had loan spells with Hull City and Derby County before signing for Norwich in August 2011.

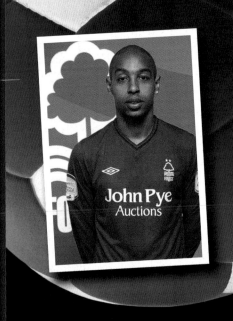

Dexter Blackstock

Position: Striker
Birthdate: 20/5/86
Nationality: Antigua and Barbuda.
Forest Appearances: 71 + 22
Forest Goals: 29

Lee Camp

Position: Goalkeeper
Birthdate: 22/8/84
Nationality: English
Forest Appearances: 165
Forest Goals: 0

He remained Forest's No 1 last season, playing in all 46 Championship games to continue his record as a virtual ever present since he arrived at The City Ground. Camp joined Forest initially on loan from Queens Park Rangers in 2008 before making the move permanent in the summer of 2009.

He won the Player of the Year award in his first full season and his excellent form led to him winning international recognition with Northern Ireland.

After suffering a sickening injury back in November 2010, Dexter finally made his return to first team action in front of the Forest faithful against Crystal Palace back in December. Dexter soon found the form which had earned him a big reputation among Forest fans. His goals towards the end of the season helped The Reds stave off relegation and also saw him receive his first International call up for his native homeland Antigua and Barbuda.

Danny Collins

Position: Defender
Birthdate: 6/8/80
Nationality: English
Forest Appearances: 0
Forest Goals: 0

The Welsh international – he has won 12 caps – was one of Sean O'Driscoll's summer recruits as Forest's new-look squad took shape. He was signed from Stoke, where he had spent three years and figured in 50 games for them in the top flight.

He started his career with Chester City before moving to Sunderland in 2004 and more than 150 appearances later he joined Stoke in 2009. He scored twice against Forest last season during a loan spell with Ipswich Town.

Chris Cohen
Position: Midfielder
Birthdate: 5/3/87
Nationality: English
Forest Appearances:
196 + 2
Forest Goals: 12

The versatile midfielder was severely missed for the majority of last season after he damaged his crucial knee ligaments during the home defeat to Derby County. Since his arrival to The City Ground in 2007 Chris has always shown he has the ability to play in a number of positions throughout the side. This was most evident in 2009 when he won the Player of the Season award.

Simon Cox
Position: Striker
Birthdate: 24/4/87
Nationality: English
Forest Appearances: 0
Forest Goals: 0

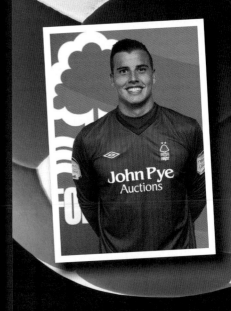

The free-scoring striker linked up with Forest in August – in a seven figure deal with West Bromwich Albion - as their seventh signing of the summer. Although he started his career with home-town Reading, it was at Swindon that he shot to limelight by scoring 32 goals in 54 league appearances and earning a £1.5m move to Albion in 2009. Although born in Reading, he was eligible to play for the Republic of Ireland through his grandmother and he has already taken his international appearances into double figures.

Karl Darlow
Position: Goalkeeper
Birthdate: 8/10/90
Nationality: English
Forest Appearances:
0 + 1
Forest Goals: 0

Matt Derbyshire
Position: Striker
Birthdate: 14/4/86
Nationality: English
Forest Appearances: 8 + 8
Forest Goals: 2

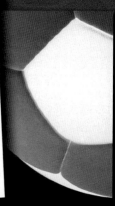

The former Blackburn striker had a disappointing first season at The City Ground, starting only seven league games and will be out to make an impression.
He first made his name with Blackburn Rovers, winning England Under 21 recognition along the way as he emerged as one of the country's top young strikers. In 2009 he moved, initially on loan, to Olympiakos in Greece and played with them in the Champions League before returning to England on loan with Birmingham City.

The highly-promising young goalkeeper made his league debut for The Reds in 2010-11 when he replaced Lee Camp for the last 15 minutes of a game against Crystal Palace.
Last season he moved to Newport County on loan to gather vital experience and figured in eight games for the Welsh club.
But with Camp's understudy Paul Smith leaving the club in 2012, Karl will be looking to establish himself as the recognised No. 2.

Robbie Findley
Position: Striker
Birthdate: 4/8/85
Nationality: American
Forest Appearances: 14 + 15
Forest Goals: 6

The American striker, who played for his country in the 2010 World Cup, showed glimpses of class during last season but ongoing injury niggles restricted the former Real Salt Lake player to a limited number of first team appearances.
Despite the lack of first team matches Robbie managed six goals in just 14 appearances, three of which came in the cup matches against Notts County, Wycombe and Newcastle United.

PLAYER PROFILES

Simon Gillett
Position: Midfield
Birthdate: 6/11/85
Nationality: English
Forest Appearances: 0
Forest Goals: 0

He was snapped up by manager Sean O'Driscoll following his release from Doncaster, where they were together for a couple of years. O'Driscoll had, in fact, taken the neat and tidy midfielder from his first club Southampton to Rovers, where he became a regular over the following two seasons.

In his time he has had loan spells with Walsall, Blackpool (twice), Bournemouth and Yeovil as well as Doncaster but is now striving to find a permanent slot in a Forest side pushing for promotion.

Adlene Guedioura
Position: Midfield
Birthdate: 12/11/85
Nationality: Algerian
Forest Appearances: 19
Goals: 1

The Algerian midfielder was an instant hit when he first arrived at The City Ground last season on loan from Wolves. His energy and ball-playing skills quickly endeared him to Forest fans and he earned further acclaim at the end of the season when he won the Goal of the Season award for his spectacular strike in the 7-3 win at Leeds in March. He returned to Wolves at the end of the season but, much to the delight of his new fans in Nottingham, his move to The City Ground was made permanent in July.

Jonathan Greening
Position: Midfielder
Birthdate: 2/1/79
Nationality: English
Forest Appearances: 29 + 7
Forest Goals: 0

Greg Halford

Position: Defender
Birthdate: 8/12/84
Nationality: English
Forest Appearances: 0
Forest Goals: 0

The experienced defender was Forest's fourth signing of last summer, joining The Reds in a deal from troubled Portsmouth.

He first made his name as an attacking full back with Colchester, playing 150 league games for them before moving to Reading. After a short spell with them, he signed for Sunderland in 2007 and then Wolves two years later.

Greg, who can play as a central defender or right back, originally joined Portsmouth on loan and last season was second in their scoring charts.

The highly-experienced midfield man was signed from Fulham before the start of last season as a key figure in Steve McClaren's rebuilding programme.

He arrived at The City Ground having played for clubs like Manchester United, Middlesbrough, West Brom and Fulham and during his time at Boro was called into the England squad.

He began his career with York City and his impressive CV includes captaining West Brom to the Championship title in 2008.

Dan Harding

Position: Defender
Birthdate: 23/12/83
Nationality: English
Forest Appearances: 0
Forest Goals: 0

The former England Under 21 international was signed from Southampton last summer after helping the Saints surge to promotion to the Premier League.

His earlier career was spent with Brighton, Leeds and Ipswich before joining Southampton in July 2009 as Alan Pardew's first signing.

His arrival at The City Ground fills a problem left back position, which had been previously occupied by loan signings and players operating out of their accustomed roles.

Sam Hutchinson
Position: Defender
Birthdate: 3/9/89
Nationality: English
Forest Appearances: 0
Forest Goals: 0

The talented young Chelsea defender moved to The City Ground in the summer in a season-long loan deal from Stamford Bridge.

At one time it looked as though his career would be over in its infancy when he suffered a serious knee injury but he made a remarkable recovery to resurrect his footballing dreams.

He can operate as a right back or central defender and his talents were recognised earlier in his career when he was chosen for England at Under 18 and Under 19 level.

Henri Lansbury
Position: Midfield
Birthdate: 12/10/90
Nationality: English
Forest appearances: 0
Forest goals: 0

The 21 year old midfielder joined Forest last August in a four-year deal from Arsenal.

In the previous two seasons he had had lengthy loan spells with Norwich City and Birmingham City, helping both of them win promotion to the Premier League. Earlier in his career Henri also had a successful loan spell with Scunthorpe United, who he also helped to win promotion. In addition to his club career he has also represented England at all levels leading up to the Under 21s.

Jamaal Lascelles
Position: Defender
Birthdate: 11/11/93
Nationality: English
Forest Appearances: 1
Forest Goals: 0

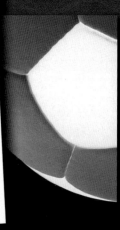

Radoslaw Majewski

Position: Midfielder
Birthdate: 15/12/86
Nationality: Polish
Forest Appearances: 85 + 16
Forest Goals: 13

'Radi', as he is known to his team mates, struggled to nail down a permanent role within the team last season but made an increasing impact in the second half of the campaign.

However, the former Polish International did stake a claim for performance of the season with his stunning hat-trick display against Crystal Palace which earned the Reds a vital 3 points away from home.

One of the game's most talked about young defenders, he looks to be on the threshold of an impressive career in the game.

He was handed his first team debut against Burnley last season and then moved to Stevenage on loan to make a big impression in their bid for promotion from League One.

Jamaal has also made strides on the international scene, representing England at Under 18 and Under 19 level.

David McGoldrick

Position: Striker
Birthdate: 29/11/87
Nationality: English
Forest Appearances: 36 + 38
Forest Goals: 10

The Nottingham-born striker has made only six league starts over the last two seasons in what has been a frustrating time for him. He arrived at the club from Southampton in 2009 and although he has struggled throughout that time to hold down a regular place, he remains a player of rich potential. David began his career with Notts County before moving to Southampton, where he scored 14 league and cup goals in the season before he moved to The City Ground.

Lewis McGugan
Position: Midfield
Birthdate: 25/10/88
Nationality: English
Forest Appearances: 146 + 49
Forest Goals: 36

The talented midfielder, a product of the club's Academy system, made his debut in the 2006-07 and has been a member of the first team squad ever since.

He scored 13 goals in the 2010-11 season – his most productive – and his ability to produce spectacular strikes have been a trademark feature of his game. Added to that the Nottingham-born player's skill on the ball has made him a big crowd favourite at The City Ground.

Brendan Moloney
Position: Defender
Birthdate: 18/1/89
Nationality: Irish
Forest Appearances: 23 + 10
Forest Goals: 0

The young Irishman came through Forest's youth system to make his debut in the 2006-07 season and he has always shown rich potential.

His lack of first team opportunities at The City Ground have led to a succession of loan moves to Chesterfield, Rushden & Diamonds, Notts County and Scunthorpe.

But many judges believe he is more than capable of holding down a regular first team place with The Reds and that will be his aim in a new-look set-up.

Guy Moussi
Position: Midfield
Birthdate: 23/1/85
Nationality: French
Forest Appearances: 102 + 14
Forest Goals: 3

Andy Reid
Position: Midfielder
Birthdate: 29/7/82
Nationality: Irish
Forest Appearances: 160 + 43
Forest Goals: 26

The creative midfielder's return to The City Ground – he left for Tottenham in 2005 - was a tale of two halves. The first half of the season saw the former Republic of Ireland international struggle to hold down a first team place. However, he produced a match-winning display away to Ipswich which saw the Reds end an unwanted goalless streak with a 3-1 win. The winger's performances improved as the season progressed and he soon became a regular in the team.

The popular French midfielder moved to Forest from SCO Angers in his native country after playing 120 games for them over a six-year period.

He wasted no time in making a big impact at The City Ground but a serious knee ligament injury brought an abrupt end to his first season and he was out of action for five months.

But he returned to the fold and signed a new contract at the club in 2011 after several Premier League clubs had shown an interest in signing him.

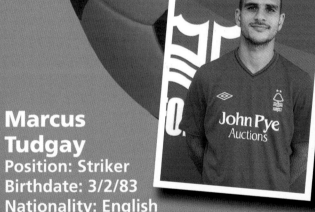

Marcus Tudgay
Position: Striker
Birthdate: 3/2/83
Nationality: English
Forest Appearances: 46 + 16
Forest Goals: 13

The former Derby County and Sheffield Wednesday front man had an unhappy start to last season when he didn't figure in former manager Steve McLaren's plans.

But he returned to the first team to show flashes of the form that made him a respected striker with his former clubs, scoring twice in a crucial 3-1 win over Ipswich.

He joined Forest in January 2011 after scoring 50 goals in just over 200 appearances for Wednesday.

45

FOREST HISTORY

Nottingham Forest have a long and proud tradition that has brought major success on the field while producing a brand of football that is pleasing on the eye.

Ever since the club was formed in 1865 it has upheld a belief to play the game in the 'right' way with quality football and sportsmanship as important to them as the pursuit of silverware.

Never were those factors put into context more than the remarkable years in which Brian Clough was manager of the club and put the name of Nottingham Forest into the forefront of European and World sport.

Clough spent 18 years at the club from 1975-1993 and it was a period that led to the master manager taking on legendary status as he inspired Forest to huge levels of success on the field.

When he took over, Forest were a struggling side in the second tier of English football but within two and a half years they were promoted to the top division and a further 12 months down the line they were champions of England.

That was only the start of Forest's achievements as they qualified for European competition and, against all odds and predictions, they went on to become European Champions in 1979 and 1980, defeating Swedish side Malmo 1-0 in Munich and following up with another 1-0 success against Hamburg, of Germany, in Madrid.

Those successes stand out as the high spots in the club's history and

to this day the name of Nottingham Forest is instantly recognised all over Europe for those glorious years. Other major domestic honours – Forest were four times winners of the Football League Cup during Clough's reign – served to underline the club's identity as one of England's leading clubs.

The name of Clough will be forever linked with Forest's successful times and rightly so but outside of his never-to-be-forgotten years in charge, Forest have known other times of great joy.

None more so than in 1959 when they won the FA Cup after defeating Luton Town 2-1 at Wembley despite the fact that they had been reduced to ten men when one of their goalscorers Roy Dwight was stretchered off the field with a broken leg.

That followed their other FA Cup success in 1898, when they defeated arch rivals Derby County 3-1 at Crystal Palace.

In 1967 Forest were so close to huge achievements in both league

and cup when they boasted one of the most attractive footballing sides of any generation under the management of Johnny Carey.

Unfortunately the qualities that they had in abundance went unrewarded when they finished as runners-up to Manchester United in the race for the then First Division championship and were beaten by Tottenham Hotspur in the semi final of the FA Cup at Hillsborough.

Many other Forest teams have been close to major honours down the years since the club was formed by a group of 'shinney' players.

That was a game that resembled hockey more than football but at a special meeting in Nottingham, a motion was passed to switch from 'shinney' to football and in 1886 Forest played their first game against city neighbours Notts County.

In their early years Forest celebrated a number of 'firsts' in the game … the first time any team had worn shin guards in 1874; playing the first game in which a referee's whistle was used in 1878

and the first time that any team had adopted a classical formation of a goalkeeper, two full backs, three-man half back line and five forwards.

The club also had several 'homes' during their formative years, starting with the Forest Racecourse, where they stayed until 1879. They moved on at regular intervals to the Castle Ground, the Meadows, Trent Bridge, the Parkside Ground, Gregory Ground and then eventually to The City Ground in 1897. The club have resided at The City Ground, by the banks of the river Trent, ever since.

Although Forest at times attracted huge crowds and won admirers for the purist element in their play, they were never close to major success until the 1959 Wembley win under Billy Walker.

The 1960s and the Clough era put Forest into the forefront of the game and even though Clough retired in 1993, his successor Frank Clark led the club back into the Premier League, a third place finish and qualification for European football. That was no mean achievement but after he departed in 1996 there followed a period in which Forest were relegated,

promoted and relegated again from the top flight of English football.

Their last demotion from the Premier League was in 1999 and the club suffered further problems in 2005 when they slipped into League One.

By that time Nigel Doughty had taken over as owner of the club and in 2008 Forest was promoted back into the Championship and in 2010 and 2011 were involved in the play-offs to get into the Premier League but experienced disappointment on both occasions. But the dream remains that one day soon Forest will once more take their place at the top table of English football.

NEW OWNERS/ NEW KIT

There can't have been many occasions in the history of football when a new kit was unveiled on the same day as the club's new owners were announced. Well, it happened at Forest in 2012! On Saturday July 14, Abdul Aziz, Fawaz and Omar Al Hasawi were in town after buying The Reds. Some people had flown all the way from the Middle East just to meet them. Everyone was excited. Fans, desperate to catch a glimpse of the men who promised to bring the glory days back to The City Ground, crowded into the car park.

It seemed to take an age for them to appear, but when they did - what an atmosphere! Supporters chanted and clamoured to shake hands with the three men and there was an air of excitement surrounding the entire day. Before everyone knew it, the Al Hasawis' were inside speaking to journalists from all over the world.

There was even a man from Kuwait, whose microphone was so big it covered half of Fawaz's face. One journalist asked if Forest could become similar to super-rich Manchester City. "We would like to be!" replied Abdul Aziz. "We have ambitions, we have hopes and, some day we will probably play against Manchester City and Manchester United."

Afterwards, 100 lucky fans got to meet the new owners in person. Even world-champion boxer Carl Froch was there to show his support. On the same day, fans were treated to their first glimpse of The Reds' brand new home strip. Designed by Umbro, who also make England's kits, its stylish design and use of Forest's famous Garibaldi red made it a kit fit for the Premier League - and Forest were only one promotion away from making the dream a reality.

CROSSWORD

ACROSS

1. French central midfielder.
4. England cricketer and Forest fan, Stuart ....
7. Only ever-present player in all Championship games last season.
8. Centre back - went on loan to Stevenage at the end of last season, Jamaal ....
9. Scored a hat-trick in The Reds' 3-0 away win against Crystal Palace.
10. Hard working centre forward.
13. Midfielder sorely missed through injury last season.
14. Stand behind the River Trent.
16. The Reds beat this team 7-3 last season.
17. American centre forward.

DOWN

1. Robin Hood and Maid ....
2. Forest beat this team 2-0 in the final game of last season.
3. Striker who came back from a long-term injury grabbing us 8 goals after Christmas.
5. Young defender who moved to Derby last August.
6. Famous Forest manager, Brian ....
11. Joined us on loan from Wolves last season and instantly became a fan's favourite.
12. Former Forest goalkeeper, Paul ....
13. Former Forest manager.
15. Reds striker signed from West Brom last season.

Answers on P61.

PLAYER FACTS

DEXTER BLACKSTOCK

- He was born in Oxford on May 20, 1986.
- His full name is Dexter Anthony Titus Blackstock.
- He was a youth player with Oxford United.
- He made his debut in league football with Southampton in 2003.
- He played more than 100 league games for Queens Park Rangers before joining Forest.
- He has played for England at Under 18, 19 and 21 level.
- He once played in goal for Southampton in 2006 after they had used all their substitutes.
- He won his first cap for Antigua and Barbuda in February 2012.
- Earlier in his playing career he had loan spells with Derby County and Plymouth Argyle.
- He had 12 months out of the game after sustaining a serious knee injury in November 2010.

FAVOURITES:

Ground: Old Trafford
Player: Ronaldo
Sportsman: Michael Jordan
Food: Garlic prawns
Car: Rolls Royce Phantom
TV Programme: 24
Film: The Usual Suspects
Album: The Blueprint – JAY-Z
Place to visit: Los Angeles
Game played in: Bristol City, April 2009

GOAL OF THE SEASON

Adlene Guedioura may only have spent three months at The City Ground last season but he still found time to produce a magical and memorable moment.

The Algerian international swooped Wolves' unsuccessful bid to stay in the Premier League to lend his considerable skills to our successful Championship survival mission.

He made 19 appearances while on loan with us and his twinkling midfield displays quickly made him a favourite of the fans.

Guedioura scored just once but his goal not only kick-started our seven-goal demolition of Leeds but also landed him a top award.

The goal at Elland Road – a fiercely struck shot from 30 yards that deceived goalkeeper Andy Lonergan before dipping under the crossbar – earned him the club's official Goal of the Season award.

And Guedioura admits he will never forget his super strike - or the brief spell he spent as a Red.

He says: "I loved my time as a Forest player because everyone, from the manager, the players, coaching staff, kit-man and fans, made me so welcome.

"That meant an awful lot to me – I felt honoured by the way people accepted me straight away and made me feel a big part of the club.

"I just wanted to play first team football again because I was not getting that opportunity at Wolves.

"Forest is a wonderful club and it filled me with so much satisfaction that we were able to climb away from the relegation zone."

The 7-3 win over Leeds at Elland Road certainly boosted confidence in our dressing room and Steve Cotterill's men hardly looked back after that incredible night.

Guedioura says: "I will never forget the Leeds game. It was incredible to go there and play so well and score seven goals.

"Everyone was on a high after that. It was a huge result for us and gave us even more belief.

"I was delighted to play my part with a goal. People know that I like to shoot whenever I get the opportunity – sometimes it doesn't work out but on that occasion it did.

"I caught the ball really sweetly and it was a fantastic feeling when it hit the back of the net.

"I was honoured to win the Goal of the Season award. I'm very grateful to the fans who voted for me and I'll always treasure it.

"I've been asked whether it was the best goal of my career but I scored one for Wolves like that and also one for Algeria that was the same, so I will let other people judge."

Nottingham Forest's official website led the way when it was launched 15 years ago – and it's still No. 1 now.

NEW WEBSITE

www.nottinghamforest.co.uk was the first football club website in the UK to broadcast live commentary on a match-day. That was on January 28, 1998 when internet listeners were able to tune in and hear The Reds beat Queen's Park Rangers 1-0 at Loftus Road, thanks to a late goal from central defender Colin Cooper.

Such innovation and forward thinking soon made the website, which had been created a year earlier by Geoff Peabody and backed by Forest's late owner Nigel Doughty, an enormous success – and the template for other clubs to follow.

In 2004 the site was named Website of the Year at the glittering Football League Awards ceremony in London.

And even now it's the most visited website in the Football League, attracting an average of 288,000 unique visitors per month as well as an average of 2.5million page views.

Forest Player – a subscription-based web TV service, which features daily star interviews, full match highlights, match commentary and re-runs of classic matches – boasts more than 5,000 subscribers, which is also the highest in the league.

Commentary is provided by BBC Radio Nottingham's top team, which includes Forest's ex-captain John McGovern, the man who had the honour of lifting the European Cup in 1979 and 1980.

The Reds have followers all over the world and supporters in Scandinavia, Ireland, Australia, USA and Canada keep abreast of developments at The City Ground via the website and Forest Player.

In the early days of the website, a fan even used to listen to commentary from base camp at Antarctica.

The website underwent a revamp during the summer of 2012 and was re-launched with a whole new look.

But the aim of the site remains the same: to keep fans of the club abreast with official club news, big name interviews and the very best in match-day coverage.

Website Manager Aldo Turner says: "The website is a fantastic communication tool for Nottingham Forest and also generates a great deal of money for the club.

"Along with the income from Forest Player, the club earns a percentage of the online TV rights sold by the Football League based on the amount of subscribers to Forest Player - so the more successful the website is results in a bigger slice of the pie.

"We are very proud to have the most visited club website in the Football League.

"It's a reward for the hard work that has been put in over the past 15 years but we wouldn't be where we are without the superb following of the Forest fans."

PLAYER FACTS

ANDY REID

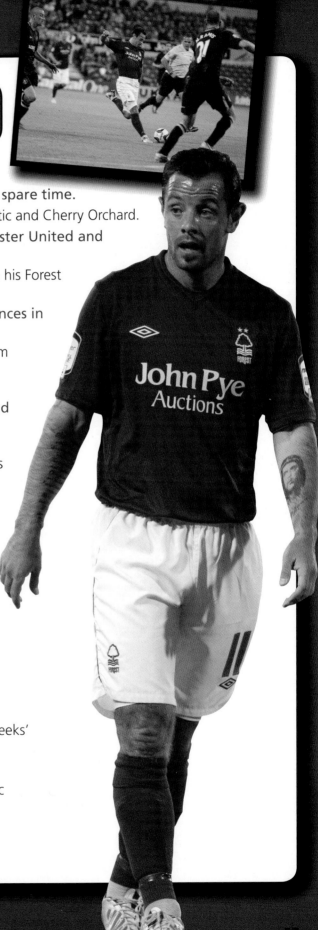

- His middle name is Matthew.
- He enjoys playing the guitar in his spare time.
- He began his career with Lourdes Celtic and Cherry Orchard.
- He had the chance to join Manchester United and Arsenal as a youngster.
- He scored against Sheffield United on his Forest debut in 2000.
- He scored 21 goals in 144 appearances in his first spell with Forest.
- He left Forest for Tottenham in an £8m package deal with central defender Michael Dawson.
- When he signed for Forest a second time he was Steve McClaren's first signing for the club.
- In the 2003-04 season he was Forest's top scorer with 13 goals.
- He's won 24 Republic of Ireland caps at senior level.

FAVOURITES:

Ground: White Hart Lane

Player: Paul Scholes

Sportsman: Brian O'Driscoll

Food: Irish stew

Car: Porsche 911

TV Programme: Entourage

Film: Good Will Hunting

Album: Either Van Morrison's 'Astral Weeks' or Bob Dylan's 'Blood on the Tracks'

Place to visit: Bahamas

Game played in: v Holland for Republic of Ireland in June 2004

TRAINING GROUND

We proudly boast one of the most impressive and stylish training facilities in English football.

For many years past managers and players took the long walk from The City Ground along the River Trent to eventually reach the Holme Road training ground.

All that changed in 2011, however, when a brand new state of the art training complex was built on Wilford Road, West Bridgford. Funded by the late former Forest owner Nigel Doughty, the manager and players are now able to enjoy Premiership standard facilities throughout the season.

The striking two-storey building includes the latest high tech equipment and facilities which are required to meet the demands of a modern day footballer. The complex even has an indoor facility for the players to use during the more severe winter months.

During the weekends the next generation of Forest players use the site which has eight full size pitches available, all of which are fully maintained all year round.

The impressive facilities include the following:

Gym
There is a fully equipped gym which includes a unique 'anti gravity machine' which was specially added to help long term injured players along their road to recovery. This has been of incredible benefit to players like Dexter Blackstock and Chris Cohen, who have returned to action after long lay-offs following knee surgery.

Changing Rooms
Each player has a designated locker with their own security code and a couple of ice baths are on hand for

the team to help them wind down after a hard day's training. It might not be the most popular part of the complex but there's nothing like an ice bath to help those tired legs!

Restaurant/Canteen

It is important for a modern day footballer to have a balanced diet, which is why the players have a specialised chef, who prepares breakfast and lunch for the management and players. If you want to find one of the players in their break times you can bet they are in the canteen playing table tennis, which, outside of football, is the most popular activity on the training ground.

Media Room

Members of the local and national media will base themselves in the media room on press days. It's where they interview the manager and players ahead of forthcoming matches. There is a specially constructed backdrop, which is used for interviews and coverage on TV.

Manager's Office

The manager has his own private room in the complex, overlooking the training pitches so he can keep an eye on what's happening – even when he's on the telephone!

Meeting Room

The manager, coaching staff and players regularly congregate in the meeting room to talk tactics ahead of matches. The room is equipped with a tactics board and over head projector, so the players can watch previous matches and study upcoming opponents.

Page 10
Who am I?
Dexter Blackstock, Chris Cohen, Guy Moussi and Andy Reid

Pages 16 and 17
Forest Quiz
1 Garath McCleary
2 Wes Morgan
3 Jonathan Greening
4 Frank Clark
5 Steve McClaren
6 Chris Cohen
7 Paul Smith
8 Wales
9 FC Twente
10 Greg Cunningham, Adlene Guedioura, George Elokobi, Danny Higginbotham, Scott Wootton
11 Portsmouth
12 Polish
13 Chris Gunter
14 Dexter Blackstock (2) and Adlene Guedioura
15 Lee Camp
16 Garath McCleary
17 Trevor Francis and John Robertson
18 Swansea City
19 West Bromwich Albion
20 The Brian Clough Stand

Page 30
Wordsearch

A	B	C	C	I	T	Y	G	R	O	U	N	D	C	N	E
K	L	I	B	D	R	E	A	D	A	A	O	I	I	A	S
I	A	T	D	I	E	R	R	U	E	K	D	W	T	I	H
I	C	G	S	R	N	D	T	G	D	R	G	I	Y	R	A
S	K	D	A	T	T	M	O	R	U	I	E	P	M	A	C
B	S	A	L	Y	E	N	S	P	G	N	R	L	G	M	R
L	T	O	K	B	N	O	I	M	O	B	I	L	E	R	D
A	O	N	M	A	D	I	D	N	U	L	S	F	E	O	H
C	C	L	O	U	G	H	E	L	T	U	D	G	A	Y	A
K	K	Z	U	W	G	V	Y	H	I	F	A	I	Z	B	C
F	P	M	S	E	H	T	M	G	O	B	L	N	E	I	D
G	I	N	S	F	E	R	D	R	U	C	R	D	R	N	C
T	I	F	I	N	D	L	E	Y	R	K	A	O	L	T	O
R	A	O	T	N	R	S	W	D	O	Y	D	Y	B	A	H
A	M	E	C	U	T	A	Q	E	B	E	K	O	D	I	E
E	L	E	B	W	N	M	A	J	E	W	S	K	I	K	N

Page 30
Spot the Difference

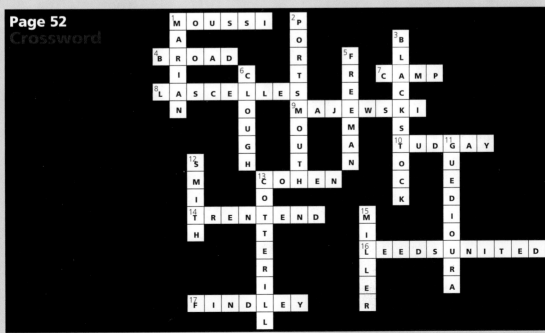

Page 52
Crossword

1 MOUSSI 2 P
4 BROAD 5 F 3 B
7 CAMP
8 LASCELLES
6 C 9 MAJEWSKI
10 TUDGAY 11 G
12 S 13 COHEN
14 TRENTEND 15 M
16 LEEDSUNITED
17 FINDLEY

WHERE'S ROBIN?